A Funeral For Our Butterflies

Vanessa Clairmont

(c) 2018 Vanessa Clairmont. All rights reserved. No part of this publication may be reproduced, in whole or in part, in any format, without prior written permission from the copyright holder.

Dedicated to the man who gave me the best and the worst of life. You were my life's greatest lesson.

CHAPTERS

Chapter One
You & I

Chapter Two
Saboteur

Chapter Three
Dead Butterflies

Chapter Four
New

Chapter One

You & I

your promises
were too good
to be true

i should have seen that
from the start

i remember looking at your face
and feeling only one thing:
desire.

now i look at photos of us
and wonder how
i was so blind
that i couldn't see
what was right in front of me…

you made me feel safe
when i felt as if
the whole world
was against me

the first of our butterflies
hatched from the cocoon
young and idyllic
too pure to know
that love is only
disappointment
and
pain.

i have to give you credit
for teaching me
that no one
is as they seem

my heart is a traitor
for it loves a man
who did nothing
but hurt me

your words
dripped
like honey
with sweetness
and affection

never give your heart to someone
who refuses to treat it
with kindness and love

there is nothing like
new memories
to make you forget
those who hurt you

i am valuable.

despite your every effort
to tell me otherwise
i am valuable
and there is nothing
you can do
to change that.

i thought that if i
was a sunflower
you were the water
that nourished me

but now i see
you never gave me
anything
but poison.

tear down the walls between us.

    let's make it right
       and try
    to start again.

if i could get on a plane
tomorrow
and start a whole new life
with no trace
of your memory
believe me, i would

every time you say her name
i feel a new wound bleeding
in my heart

find someone
who is willing
to reassure you
no matter what.

if you're just in it when its easy
you're not really in it
at all.

i admit that i mistook
the way you lusted for me
for real attraction

i wish i could've seen
who you were
and what you really wanted
before it was too late.

if they don't care enough
to text you back
and reassure you
that they care

they're just not worth it.

i fell too fast

you laughed
as i drowned

you never cared about me
you only cared
about what you could get from me.

never settle for a man
who only wants one thing

weak men are afraid of powerful women.
powerful men aren't afraid— they're
entranced.

was there nothing real
about your promises?
was it all
nothing but lies?

Chapter Two

Saboteur

you convinced me
we were on the same side
but you waited
until the moment was right
and stabbed me in the back

please, god
let me never think of him again.

don't settle for someone
who doesn't truly listen
to what you have to say

if he doesn't listen
to what you have to say
your ever word is wasted.

broken hearts
bleeding as one
we all understand
the pain.

sometimes you have to admit
that it's time to give up.

some
people
relationships
situations

are just too toxic to keep around.

you were never in love with me
you were just lonely.

everything i thought
about who you were
was wrong.

you would do and say
anything
to get what you wanted

and i, like a fool
ate up every morsel
of affection
lacking the wisdom
to separate lust from attraction.

some people
can't be saved

and there's no use trying
until they save themselves.

every tear
you made me cry
every kiss
i wasted on you

each one was a lesson
that i will never forget.

never settle for a man
who thinks he needs
multiple women
in order to be happy

it just means that he
doesn't think
that you
are enough

but
never forget
that you are
more than enough.

i wish i could tell my heart
what my mind already knows:
you were never worth it

and yet still, my heart yearns
like a fool
for your touch

we went through hell together
it's a shame you never suffered
as much as i did

a path of rose petals
from the door to your bed
lit candles
a false apology

but i can't say no
and here i am
next to you
in your bed

i can never say no
to you
and that
is my greatest weakness.

why does everyone
have to leave?

if he tries to pressure you
to do things
you don't want to do
or aren't ready for

he doesn't want you
he just wants to use you.

as i let you go
i knew i was letting go
of the best
and worst
thing
i've ever had.

take yourself out
for a night of fun

forget him
forget your troubles

you deserve
to be happy.

i get attached too easily
i love too hard, too fast

but i can't believe
i was dumb enough to believe you
when you said
"i love you".

why is it so hard
to let go
of someone
so obviously toxic?

i need you
to save me
from myself

if he gets angry
when you tell him
how you feel

he doesn't care
about you

your love
was poisoned chocolate

tasting so sweet
but hurting so terribly.

i will never get an explanation
from you
for why i wasn't good enough
and it's time
i accepted that

i only wish
that you loved me
the way
i love you

if he lets you
go to bed
upset

he doesn't care
about you

i wish i wasn't so good
at ruining
good things

Chapter Three

Dead Butterflies

rest in peace
to all the butterflies
that used to flutter
at every word you spoke
and every time you smiled

how fitting;
you never did want me
to spread my wings
and fly away.

there is no greater feeling
than finally letting go
of someone
whose smile
used to haunt your waking moments
and pervade your dreams

freedom, to me
means finally
letting go
of you.

i only wish
i had more time
on this earth

love is not
a series
of grand gestures

love is listening
to how you day went
love is kissing your forehead
and not just making out

love is the small things.

i'm sorry, but i cannot accept
your apology.

i could never cause myself
so much pain.

we were always fighting
that should've been
my first clue.

i wish i could take
a handful of balloons
and float away
to another place
and start
a new life

it's important
to see the beautiful
in everything in life

it's easy to get caught up
in the horrors of the news
or mundanity of daily life
but take heart, and do not forget
there is beauty everywhere
if only you care to look.

if you're wondering
if it's time to move on

it is.

the question is answered
in the fact that it is asked.

i can't say that i regret
our time together
for although it hurt
more than anything
it also taught me
more lessons
than anything else.

never beg someone
to be part of your life.

if you have to beg them,
they don't deserve
your time, love, or energy.

stop holding on
to things of the past

there is no use
in re-opening old wounds
that could've healed long ago
if you left them alone

i traced a finger
along your freckles
as if i was tracing constellations
in the stars

being neglected
is a terrible burden
that no one should have to bear.

it is a terrible thing
to be taught
that you are not worth
someone's time
or love.

if you love someone
just tell them

life is short
there's no use
in missing out
on living it to the fullest.

there is no greater feeling
than knowing
that you're doing just fine
without someone
who you used to need.

your time is too valuable
to waste
on people
who can't make up their mind
if they want you or not

it's okay to protect your heart
and refuse to take chances on people
who are just going to let you down

if you have something nice to say
about someone
reach out and say it

nothing spreads joy in the world
like unexpected compliments

do me a favor
and leave me alone
if you're only planning
on using me
and breaking my heart.

the greatest struggle
of getting over someone
is staying strong
keeping your mind off of them
and suddenly
out of the blue
something reminds you of them
and suddenly
you're hurting
all over again

you can't tell people to leave
and then blame them
for leaving

Chapter Four

New

the river
will bend
and life
will change

hold on
you have more
to live for

don't fall in love
with people
who are still in love
with someone else

all they're doing
is looking
for pieces of who they want
in you

watch how
they treat
people around them;

workers

family

strangers

if they don't treat
those around them
in a good way

run away

your smile
is the most beautiful sunrise

you are the only one
you need

don't settle for anything
or anyone

you deserve
better
than you can possibly
imagine

sometimes you have to accept
that you'll never get an answer
about why it ended

though we feel we need
closure
sometimes we must accept
that we'll never get it

i would rather be alone
than be loved by a man
who doesn't truly care about me

be wise
and do not settle
for anyone
who doesn't love you
wholly and completely

there is nothing more powerful
than a woman
who is fully aware
of everything
she deserves

new beginnings
are a chance
to change yourself

you deserve to be loved
as if you have no past
and don't carry the weight
of past failed loves

nothing hurts quite as much
as someone telling you
they love you
and then leaving

i am finally ready
to move on
and find a new love

one that won't leave me
or hurt me

i will find someone
to love me
in all the ways
you never could

i am addicted to the idea
that we could've been
something truly magical

sometimes you just have to accept
that the one you want
just isn't the right one
for you.

don't settle for anything less
than total and complete
happiness

i have finally found someone
who won't hurt me
or lie to me

i have finally allowed my heart
the freedom
to love someone
who deserves me

i know i will never forget you
or what we had together
but one day
i will finally forget
the desperate longing
i once felt
to be loved by you

and on that day
i will be truly free.

i wake up and step outside
letting the sun hit my face
and a gentle breeze
flow through my open hands

i realize that i did not
dream of you
for the first time
in so long

and i smile.

the old butterflies are dead
but finally
new, young ones are born
and i can love again
at last.